FCAT Writing+ for Grade 8: Strands, Standards, and Benchmc

Strand: Writing

Standard 1: The student uses the writing process ef

LA.B.1.3.1. The student organizes information befoɪ
according to the type and purpose of writing.

Benchmark Clarifications

Focus

Clarification 1.3.1.1. The student demonstrates
knowledge of the function of planning in accomplishing
the specific writing mode or purpose.

Clarification 1.3.1.2. The student recognizes how
modifications to a writing plan affect the maintenance of
the writing focus.

Organization

Clarification 1.3.1.3. The student demonstrates knowledge of the function of prewriting in establishing an effective organizational plan.

LA.B.1.3.2. The student drafts and revises writing that is focused, purposeful, and reflects insight into the writing situation; conveys a sense of completeness or wholeness with adherence to the main idea; has an organizational pattern that provides for a logical progression of ideas; has support that is substantial, specific, relevant, concrete, and/or illustrative; demonstrates a commitment to and an involvement with the subject; has clarity in presentation of ideas; uses creative writing strategies appropriate to the purpose of the paper;

demonstrates a command of language (word choice) with freshness of expression; has varied sentence structure and sentences that are complete except when fragments are used purposefully; and has few, if any, convention errors in mechanics, usage, and punctuation. Note: The conventions portion of this benchmark is assessed by LA.B.1.3.3. (Also assesses LA.B.2.3.3.)

Benchmark Clarifications

Focus

Clarification 1.3.2.1. The student demonstrates knowledge of effective ways to focus on a central idea or topic.

Clarification 1.3.2.2. The student demonstrates knowledge of the mode or purpose for writing.

Organization

Clarification 1.3.2.3. The student demonstrates knowledge of how a logical progression of ideas contributes to effective organization and communication.

Clarification 1.3.2.4. The student demonstrates knowledge of how to use transitional elements to develop relationships among ideas.

Support

Clarification 1.3.2.5. The student demonstrates knowledge of how to incorporate supporting ideas that clarify, explain, or define, contributing to a sense of completeness or wholeness in writing.

Clarification 1.3.2.6. The student demonstrates knowledge of how communication is affected by word choice.

LA.B.1.3.3. The student produces final documents that have been edited for correct spelling; correct punctuation, including commas, colons, and semicolons; correct capitalization; effective sentence structure; correct common usage, including subject/verb agreement, common noun/pronoun agreement, common possessive forms, and with a variety of sentence structures, including parallel structure; and correct formatting. Note: This benchmark assesses the conventions portion of LA.B.1.3.2. Correct formatting is not assessed.

Benchmark Clarifications

Conventions

Clarification 1.3.3.1. The student demonstrates knowledge of spelling conventions.

Clarification 1.3.3.2. The student demonstrates knowledge of punctuation conventions.

Clarification 1.3.3.3. The student demonstrates knowledge of correct capitalization.

Clarification 1.3.3.4. The student demonstrates knowledge of standard English usage.

Clarification 1.3.3.5. The student demonstrates knowledge of sentence structure.

1. In which sentence below is all **usage** correct?

    A. I could of gone to the game, but I got sick.
    B. I could've gone to the game, but I got sick.
    C. I couldve gone to the game, but I got sick.

Analysis:

A. Choice A is incorrect. "Could of" is a nonstandard use of the words "could have."

B. Choice B is correct. The rule of using the apostrophe for showing that letters have been omitted has been applied correctly.

C. Choice C is incorrect. The rule of using the apostrophe for showing that letters have been omitted was not applied.

2. In which sentence below is all **punctuation** correct?

   F. My dentist, says I have two cavities, because I didn't
       brush enough.

   G. My dentist says I have two cavities because I didn't
       brush enough.

   H. My dentist says I have two cavities, because I didn't
       brush enough.

Analysis:
F. Choice F is incorrect because none of the usage rules for commas are applied correctly.

G. Choice G is incorrect because the rule for the usage of a comma as a pause in a sentence is not applied.

H. Choice H is correct. This sentence shows the correct usage of commas to show a pause in a sentence.

3. In which sentence below is all **punctuation** correct?

    A. We went to the store and bought, corn broccoli and carrots for our dinner.

    B. We went to the store and bought corn, broccoli, and carrots for our dinner.

    C. We went to the store and bought corn broccoli and carrots for our dinner.

Analysis:
A. Choice A is incorrect because the usage rule for commas in a list of three or more things was not applied correctly.

B. Choice B is correct because this sentence shows the correct usage of commas for listing three of more things.

C. Choice C is incorrect because the usage rule for commas in a list of three or more things was not applied correctly.

4.   In which sentence below is all **capitalization** correct?

   F.   Juliet lives in Tallahassee, Florida.
   G.   Juliet lives in Tallahassee, florida.
   H.   Juliet lives in tallahassee, florida.

Analysis:

F. Choice F is correct because this sentence contains a geographical location. Cities and states must be capitalized.

G. Choice G is incorrect because the capitalization rules for geographical areas were not applied.

H. Choice H is incorrect because the capitalization rules for geographical areas were not applied.

5. In which sentence is all **punctuation** correct?

    A. I walked across the street to my neighbor's house for
        lunch.
    B. I walked across the street to my neighbors house, for
        lunch.
    C. I walked across the street to my neighbors house for
        lunch.

Analysis:

A. Choice A is correct. The rule for applying the apostrophe to show ownership of the "neighbor's house" is correct.

B. Choice B is incorrect because the rule for applying a comma is incorrect, and the rule for the apostrophe was not applied.

C. Choice C is incorrect because the rule for showing ownership with the apostrophe was not applied.

6.   In which sentence is all **punctuation** correct?

      F.   Jose said "Carlos, please pass the butter."
      G.   Jose, said, "Carlos, please pass the butter."
      H.   Jose said, "Carlos, please pass the butter."

Analysis:

F. Choice F is incorrect because the rule for comma usage with a quotation mark is not applied correctly.

G. Choice G is incorrect because the rule for comma usage with a quotation mark is not applied correctly.

H. Choice H is correct. This sentence shows the correct usage of a comma with quotation marks to show what someone has said directly.

Jani made the writing plan below to organize ideas for a paper. Use her writing plan to answer questions 7—9.

Jani's Writing Plan

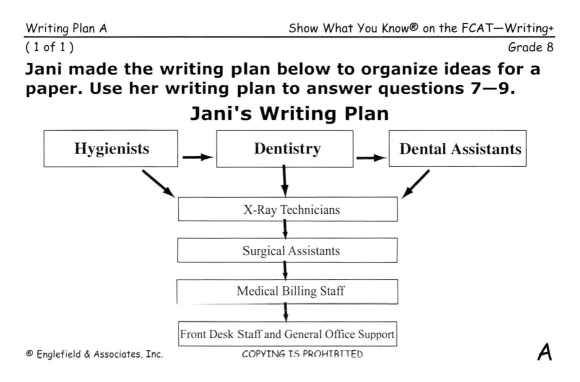

Hints for Responding to the FCAT Writing+ Questions

✔ Think positively. Some questions may seem hard, but others will be easy.

✔ Relax and do your best.

✔ Learn how to answer each kind of question. Some FCAT Writing+ multiple-choice questions have four answer choices, while others have three answer choices.

✔ Read carefully, and answer the questions you are sure about first. If a question seems too difficult, skip it, and go back to it later.

✔ Check each answer to make sure it is the best answer for the question.

7. Based on Jani's plan, what type of paper is she planning to write?

    A. a paper that persuades the reader to become a dentist
    B. a paper that gives information about the field of dentistry
    C. a paper that tells a story about a dentist
    D. a paper that gives directions to the local dentist's office

Analysis:

A. Choice A is incorrect. The plan does not include elements of persuasion such as presenting both sides of the issue.

B. Choice B is correct. The plan shows that Jani is planning to use the informational details to tell the reader about the field of dentistry.

C. Choice C is incorrect because the plan does not include the elements of fiction such as narration, characterization, setting, or plot.

D. Choice D is incorrect because the plan does not include conventional directions when using a map.

8. Based on Jani's plan, the details "greets patients," "files
    charts," and "answers phones," falls into which subtopic?

    F. Orthodontics
    G. Hygienist
    H. Front Desk Staff and General Office Support
    I. Dentistry

Analysis:

F. Choice F is incorrect. "Orthodontics" is not a subtopic.

G. Choice G is incorrect because a "Hygienist" cleans teeth.

H. Choice H is correct. The phrases "greets patients," "files charts," and "answers phones" are tasks performed by "Front Desk Staff and General Office Support."

I. Choice I is incorrect. "Dentistry" is the topic of the paper.

9. According to Jani's writing plan, which subtopic below could be added?

    A. Podiatrist
    B. Oral Surgeon
    C. Pediatrician
    D. Psychologist

Analysis:

A. Choice A is incorrect. A "Podiatrist" is a doctor that specializes in feet and does not fit with the topic.

B. Choice B is correct. An "Oral Surgeon" is a dentist with special training in surgery of the mouth.

C. Choice C is incorrect. A "Pediatrician" is a medical doctor that specializes in the treatment of children. It does not fit with the topic.

D. Choice D is incorrect. A "Psychologist" specializes in mental health issues and does not fit with the topic.

Arianna made the writing plan below to organize ideas for a paper. Use her writing plan to answer questions 10—12.

Arianna's Writing Plan

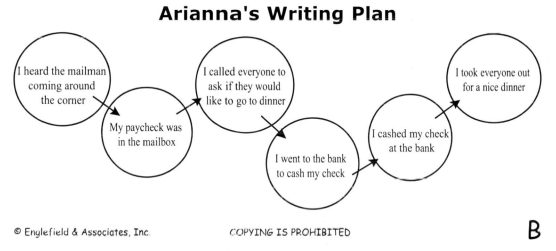

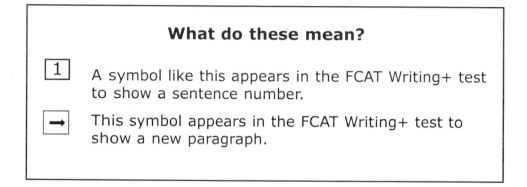

What do these mean?

1   A symbol like this appears in the FCAT Writing+ test to show a sentence number.

→   This symbol appears in the FCAT Writing+ test to show a new paragraph.

10. According to Arianna's writing plan, what is her intended
    organizational pattern?

    F. Items are presented by comparisons or contrasts listed.
    G. Items are presented in chronological order.
    H. Items are presented in a series of descriptions.
    I. Items are presented in order of least important to most
        important.

Analysis:

F. Choice F is incorrect. The plan does not include elements of comparison or contrast.

G. Choice G is correct. Arianna's plan indicates that her organizational pattern is chronological, listing the events in the order in which they happened.

H. Choice H is incorrect. The plan does not include elements of description such as sensory details.

I. Choice I is incorrect. The plan does not include elements of importance.

11. Which of the details below is repeated in the writing plan
    and should be deleted?

    A. I heard the mailman coming around the corner.
    B. My paycheck was in the mailbox.
    C. I cashed my check at the bank.
    D. I took everyone out for a nice dinner.

Analysis:

A. Choice A is incorrect. It is original information.

B. Choice B is incorrect. It is original information.

C. Choice C is correct. There are two sentences in Arianna's writing plan that state she is going to the bank.

D. Choice D is incorrect. It is original information.

12. Based on Arianna's writing plan, what kind of paper is she planning to write?

   F. a paper that persuades someone to go out to dinner
   G. a paper that informs someone of the benefits of earning a paycheck
   H. a paper that tells a story about someone who received their paycheck and then took her friends out to dinner
   I. a paper that describes how to get a check cashed

Analysis:

F.   Choice F is incorrect. There are no opinions given to influence the reader of an idea.

G.   Choice G is incorrect. There are no clues given in the plan where the writer will explain the benefits of a paycheck.

H.   Choice H is correct. Arianna's plan is narrative in nature; it describes an experience and a sequence of events which may be real or imaginative.

I.   Choice I is incorrect. There are no clues that details will be used to describe check cashing.

13. Read the sentence below:

When you graduate from high school, <u>you will knew a lot more than when you started in kindergarten.</u>

Which type of error appears in the underlined section of the sentence?

A. Usage error
B. Capitalization error
C. Punctuation error

Analysis:

A. Choice A is correct. There are usage errors in this sentence. The correct usage of the word "knew" should be "know."

B. Choice B is incorrect. There are no capitalization errors in this sentence.

C. Choice C is incorrect. There are no punctuation errors in this sentence.

14. Combine the ideas in the box to create one logical sentence.

> **an extra recess**
> **Friday afternoon**
> **earned the fifth-grade class**
> **good behavior**

Which sentence below correctly combines the ideas from the box?

F. An extra recess earned the fifth-grade class good behavior Friday afternoon.

G. Good behavior earned the fifth-grade class an extra recess Friday afternoon.

H. Friday afternoon, good behavior earned the fifth-grade class an extra recess.

Analysis:

F. Choice F is incorrect. The order of words makes the meaning of the sentence confusing.

G. Choice G is correct. This sentence correctly combines the words in the box to create a complete and meaningful sentence.

H. Choice H is incorrect. The order of words makes the meaning of the sentence confusing.

15. Read the sentence below:

**Going to the movie at 8:00 p.m. instead of
7:00 p.m. <u>ain't alright with me.</u>**

Which type of error appears in the underlined section of
the sentence?

A. Usage error
B. Capitalization error
C. Punctuation error

Analysis:

A. Choice A is correct. The use of "ain't" is unacceptable in speaking and writing, unless in quotations.

B. Choice B is incorrect because all capitalization is correct.

C. Choice C is incorrect. There are no punctuation errors in this sentence.

16. Read the sentence in the box.

The student in the library was reading a book.

Which sentence below expresses the same meaning as the sentence in the box?

F.   Reading a book, the student was in the library.
G.   In the library, the student was reading a book.
H.   The student was reading in the library a book.

Analysis:

F. Choice F is incorrect. This sentence does not clearly express the meaning of the original sentence.

G. Choice G is correct. This sentence rephrases clearly and maintains the original meaning.

H. Choice H is incorrect. This sentence does not clearly express the meaning of the original sentence.

17. Combine the ideas in the box to create one logical sentence.

> **eight chapters that day**
> **and wrote**
> **at the computer**
> **the writer sat**

Which sentence below correctly combines the ideas from the box?

A. The writer sat at the computer and wrote eight chapters that day.

B. At the computer, the writer sat, and wrote eight chapters that day.

C. Eight chapters that day, at the computer, the writer sat and wrote.

Analysis:

A. Choice A is correct. This sentence correctly combines the words in the box to create a complete and meaningful sentence.

B. Choice B is incorrect. The order of words makes the meaning of the sentence confusing.

C. Choice C is incorrect. The order of words makes the meaning of the sentence confusing.

18. In which sentence below is all **punctuation** correct?

   F.   Jeanne said, "I need to mow the grass."
   G.   Jeanne said "I need to mow the grass."
   H.   Jeanne said, "I need to mow the grass,"

Analysis:

F.   Choice F is correct. This sentence shows the correct usage of commas with quotation marks to show what someone has said directly.

G.   Choice G is incorrect because the rules for comma usage with a quotation mark are not applied correctly.

H.   Choice H is incorrect because the correct punctuation has not been used at the end of the sentence.

19. In which sentence below is all **capitalization** correct?

A. The Federal Bureau of Investigation deals with crimes
    crossing state lines.
B. The federal bureau of investigation deals with crimes
    crossing state lines.
C. The Federal Bureau of investigation deals with crimes
    crossing state lines.

Analysis:
A. Choice A is correct. This sentence capitalizes the official name of an organization, "The Federal Bureau of Investigation."

B. Choice B is incorrect because the rule of capitalizing the official name of an organization has not been applied.

C. Choice C is incorrect because the rule of capitalizing the official name of an organization has not been applied.

20. In which sentence below is all **capitalization** correct?

F. After she got cake on her dress, juanita left the room without a word.

G. After she got cake on her dress, Juanita left the room without a word.

H. After She got cake on her dress, juanita left the room without a word.

Analysis:

F. Choice F is incorrect because the rule for capitalizing proper nouns has not been applied to "Juanita."

G. Choice G is correct because the rule for capitalizing proper nouns has been applied to "Juanita."

H. Choice H is incorrect because the rule for capitalizing proper nouns has not been applied to "Juanita" and was incorrectly applied to "she."

Savannah's Writing Plan

Savannah made the writing plan on the right to organize ideas for a paper. Use her writing plan to answer questions 21—23.

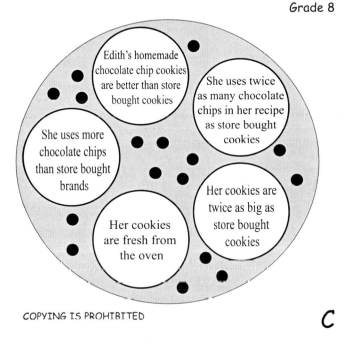

Tips for developing a Writing Plan

✔ A writing plan should be concise and simple.

✔ Avoid complete sentences whenever possible.

21. According to the writing plan, what is Savannah's intended
    organizational pattern?

    A. Items are presented by comparisons or contrasts listed.
    B. Items are presented in chronological order.
    C. Items are presented in a series of descriptions.
    D. Items are presented in order of least important to most
        important.

Analysis:

A. Choice A is correct. The writing plan indicates that Savannah's organizational pattern includes elements of comparison and contrast such as similarities and differences of store bought and homemade cookies.

B. Choice B is incorrect because the plan does not include listing events in the order in which they happened.

C. Choice C is incorrect because the plan does not include elements of description such as sensory details.

D. Choice D is incorrect because the plan does not include elements of importance.

22. Based on Savannah's plan, what type of paper is she
    planning to write?

    F.   a paper that tells a story about Edith's homemade
         cookies

    G.   a paper that explains characteristics of Edith's
         homemade cookies

    H.   a paper that gives directions on how to make Edith's
         cookies

    I.   a paper that describes the decrease in sales of store
         bought cookies

Analysis:

F. Choice F is incorrect. The plan does not include elements of narration such as character development, setting, and plot.

G. Choice G is correct because it explains the characteristics of Edith's cookies in comparison to other cookies.

H. Choice H is incorrect because the plan does not include an explanation of steps involved in making the cookies.

I. Choice I is incorrect because there is no information in the plan regarding the decrease in sales of other cookies.

23. Which of the statements in Savannah's writing plan is repeated and should be deleted?

   A. Edith's homemade chocolate chip cookies are better than store bought cookies.
   B. Her cookies are fresh from the oven.
   C. Her cookies are twice as big as store bought cookies.
   D. She uses twice as many chocolate chips in her recipe as store bought cookies.

Analysis:

A. Choice A is incorrect. It presents original information.

B. Choice B is incorrect. It presents original information.

C. Choice C is incorrect. It presents original information.

D. Choice D is correct. The statement includes information already used in the writing plan.

24. Read the sentence below:

**<u>I can't hardly wait for my sixteenth birthday</u>, because
I am getting a car from my grandparents.**

Which type of error appears in the underlined section of
the sentence?

F. Capitalization error
G. Usage error
H. Punctuation error

Analysis:
F. Choice F is incorrect. There are no capitalization errors.

G. Choice G is correct because the use of "can't hardly" is a double negative. To be stated properly, it should say, "can hardly."

H. Choice H is incorrect. There are no punctuation errors.

25. Combine the ideas in the box to create one logical sentence.

> **because the chef**
> **set the oven**
> **the cookies caught on fire**
> **temperature too high**

Which sentence below correctly combines the ideas from the box?

A. Set the oven temperature too high, because the chef, the cookies caught on fire.

B. The cookies caught on fire, because the chef temperature too high set the oven.

C. The cookies caught on fire because the chef set the oven temperature too high.

Analysis:

A. Choice A is incorrect. The order of words makes the meaning of the sentence confusing.

B. Choice B is incorrect. The order of words makes the meaning of the sentence confusing.

C. Choice C is correct. This sentence correctly combines the words in the box to create a complete and meaningful sentence.

26. In which sentence below is all **punctuation** correct?

   F.   Danielle, shut the door!
   G.   Danielle, shut the door.
   H.   Danielle, shut the door?

Analysis:

F. Choice F is correct because it demonstrates the proper application of an exclamation point as a command.

G. Choice G is incorrect because the sentence is not a statement.

H. Choice H is incorrect because the sentence does not ask a question.

The article below is a first draft that Maggie wrote. The article contains errors. Read the article to answer questions 27—31.

Monkeys and Apes

1 To fall into the primate category, you have to have fur, feed your babies milk, have the largest brains, and be warm-blooded. 2 Generally, primates do not show a significant size difference between the sexes.

D

⟶   ☐3 Monkeys are separated into New World and Old World monkeys. ☐4 Monkeys from Central and South America are New World monkeys and live exclusively in the Americas. ☐5 Old World monkeys come from Asia and Africa. ☐6 Apes come only from the Old World region. ☐7 Only they are divided into greater and lesser animals.

27. Which sentence below should Maggie add to conclude the
    article?

    A. Monkeys and Apes both fall into the primate category.
    B. Only apes fall into the primate category.
    C. Only monkeys fall into the primate category.
    D   Monkeys and apes have fur.

Analysis:

A. Choice A is correct. This idea can be concluded from the article.

B. Choice B is incorrect. Apes are not the only primates mentioned in the article and, therefore, would not make an appropriate conclusion.

C. Choice C is incorrect. Monkeys are not the only primates mentioned in the article and, therefore, would not make an appropriate conclusion.

D. Choice D is incorrect. This idea would not make a good conclusion to this article.

28. Maggie wants to add the sentence below to her article:

Another distinguishing feature of primates is fingernails, and all primates have five fingers.

Where should this sentence be added to keep the details in correct order?

F.   after sentence $\boxed{1}$

G.   after sentence $\boxed{2}$

H.   after sentence $\boxed{3}$

I.   after sentence $\boxed{4}$

Analysis:

F. Choice F is correct. Sentence ① introduces the audience to what a primate is by giving examples. This sentence adds detail to the definition of a primate by adding a few more features.

G. Choice G is incorrect. Sentence ② gives additional information only about primates to conclude the paragraph.

H. Choice H is incorrect. Sentence ③ gives information only about monkeys and not about all primates.

I. Choice I is incorrect. Sentence ④ gives information only about Old World monkeys and not about all primates.

29. Read the sentence below from Maggie's article:

---

5 **Old World monkeys come from Asia and Africa.**

Which word should replace "come" in sentence 5 to make the wording most specific?

A. start
B. originate
C. begin
D. emerge

Analysis:

A. Choice A is incorrect. "Start" is a vague answer.

B. Choice B is correct. "Originate" makes this sentence more specific by saying exactly where apes were born.

C. Choice C is incorrect. "Begin" is a vague answer.

D. Choice D is incorrect. "Emerge" would not make sense in this sentence.

30. Read the sentence below from Maggie's article:

> 6 **Only they are divided into greater and lesser animals.**

Which word(s) should replace "they" in sentence 6 to make the wording most specific?

F. apes
G. monkeys and apes
H. monkeys
I. primates

Analysis:

F. Choice F is correct. The word "apes" is correct because it is the most specific answer to replace the pronoun "they."

G. Choice G is incorrect because "monkeys and apes" is plural and "only" indicates "they" is a singular pronoun.

H. Choice H is incorrect because "monkeys" does not follow the transition of the sentence prior to it.

I. Choice I is incorrect because "primates" is not specific enough, whereas "apes" is specific enough.

31. Read the sentence below from Maggie's article:

> 4 **Monkeys from Central and South America are New World monkeys and live exclusively in the Americas.**

Which revision below improves the word choice and removes the repetition from this sentence?

A. Monkeys from the Americas are New World monkeys.

B. New World monkeys live exclusively in the Americas and Central and South America.

C. Monkeys from Central and South America are New World monkeys.

D. New World monkeys are from and live exclusively in Central and South America.

Analysis:

A. Choice A is incorrect. This version of the sentence excludes the fact that New World monkeys live exclusively in the Americas.

B. Choice B is incorrect. This has the same repetition as the original sentence. By writing "Central and South America," it is the same as saying the "Americas," so one or the other would need to be deleted.

C. Choice C is incorrect. This version of the sentence excludes the fact that New World monkeys live exclusively in the Americas.

D. Choice D is correct. This revised sentence is improved by eliminating repetition of "Central and South America" and "Americas."

Juanita made the writing plan below to organize ideas for a paper. Use her writing plan to answer questions 32—34.

Juanita's Writing Plan

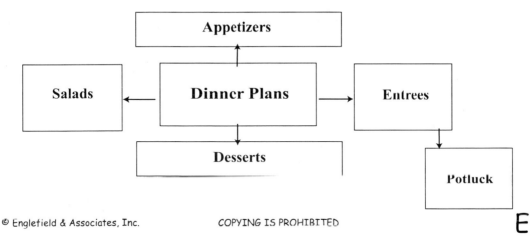

Definition: Writing Plan

Writing plans provide a prewriting structure and must have a form and style that are easy to process. Visual cues should be used to aid in processing the structure and the text. Prewriting structures may include charts, webs, diagrams, or any other grade-appropriate writing plan. Each writing plan should have a title.

32. Based on the writing plan, what type of paper is Juanita planning to write?

    F. a paper that gives information on how to throw a dinner party

    G. a paper to persuade the reader to make dinner plans

    H. a paper that tells what courses are included when making dinner plans

    I. a paper that includes instructions on how to invite friends to a party

Analysis:

F. Choice F is incorrect because the plan does not include information about throwing a dinner party.

G. Choice G is incorrect because the plan does not include elements of persuasion such as presenting both sides of the story.

H. Choice H is correct. Juanita's plan shows that she is planning on including information on courses that are most often included when making dinner plans.

I. Choice I is incorrect because the plan does not include conventional instructions on inviting friends to a party.

33. If Juanita decides to write an account of her own "dinner plans," what is the best organizational pattern for her to use?

   A.   arrange items in chronological order
   B.   arrange items in alphabetical order
   C.   arrange items in order of lightest color to darkest color
   D.   arrange items in order of largest to smallest

Analysis:

A. Choice A is correct. Chronological order presents events in time order, usually moving forward in time; also using cause and effect.

B. Choice B is incorrect. An account written in alphabetical order would not make sense for a dinner party.

C. Choice C is incorrect. An account written in order of color would not make sense for a dinner party.

D. Choice D is incorrect. Arranging the ideas from largest to smallest would not make sense for this writing plan.

34. What subtopic below would be supported by the details,
    "cookies," "brownies," and "pies"?

    F. Appetizers
    G. Desserts
    H. Salads
    I. Drinks

Analysis:

F. Choice F is incorrect because the details do not list items typically served as appetizers.

G. Choice G is correct because the details list types of desserts.

H. Choice H is incorrect because the details do not list items typically found in salads.

I. Choice I is incorrect because "drinks" is not a subtopic in Juanita's writing plan.

The report below is a first draft that George wrote for school. The report contains errors. Read the report to answer questions 35—41.

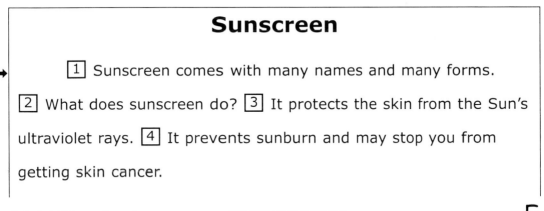

Sunscreen

1 Sunscreen comes with many names and many forms.

2 What does sunscreen do? 3 It protects the skin from the Sun's

ultraviolet rays. 4 It prevents sunburn and may stop you from

getting skin cancer.

F

→   5 Suntan lotion is different. 6 It attracts ultraviolet rays so you can become tan. 7 Consistent sun exposure causes premature skin aging.

→   8 The warnings against sun exposure can become confusing. 9 We do need certain nutrients from the sun. 10 Scientists recommend 15 minutes of direct sunlight each day. 11 The Sun is the most important source of vitamin D.

F

➡ $\boxed{12}$ The ancient Greeks were the first to use olive oil as sunscreen. $\boxed{13}$ This was not very effective. $\boxed{14}$ Many other attempts to create sunscreen during the 20th century failed. $\boxed{15}$ In 1944, during World War II, "red vet pet," was created by Ben Greene.

➡ $\boxed{16}$ As a result of Ben's invention, many advances have been made. $\boxed{17}$ We now have sunscreen in SPF 60 and water-resistant sunscreen. $\boxed{18}$ SPF stands for sun protection factor. $\boxed{19}$ There is a formula used to calculate the sunscreen SPF.

FCAT 8 Writing+

- Multiple-Choice questions are worth 1 point each
- Each writing prompt may be worth 1—6 points based upon the quality of the student's writing.

1 Expository prompt; 1 Persuasive prompt

35. Which transition should be added to the beginning of sentence ⑤ to show the connection between ideas in the report?

   A.   However
   B.   Next
   C.   Thus
   D.   Another

Analysis:

A. Choice A is correct. "However" allows for a counter example from the previous sentence.

B. Choice B is incorrect. "Next" indicates time order.

C. Choice C is incorrect. "Thus" indicates a cause/effect relationship that is not present.

D. Choice D is incorrect. "Another" indicates additional ideas are to be listed.

36. Read the sentence below from George's report:

---

4 **It prevents sunburn and may stop you from getting skin cancer.**

Which word(s) should replace "it" to make the wording most specific in sentence 4 ?

F.   Suntan lotion
G.   Sunscreen and suntan lotion
H.   Sunscreen
I.   Lotion

Analysis:

F. Choice F is incorrect. "Suntan lotion" is the incorrect information.

G. Choice G is incorrect. "Sunscreen and suntan lotion" is plural, and "it" is singular.

H. Choice H is correct. "Sunscreen" is singular and is the correct information.

I. Choice I is incorrect. "Lotion" is incorrect.

37. Which sentence below provides a detail that supports
    sentence ⬚1⬚?

    A. Names include sun block, sun cream, suntan lotion,
        and it comes in lotions, sprays, or sticks.
    B. No one knows how scientists make all of the kinds of
        sunscreen.
    C. Sunscreen lotion is the easiest to find.
    D. Sunscreen for your lips is available, also.

Analysis:

A. Choice A is correct. The sentence provides a detail that supports sentence $\boxed{1}$.

B. Choice B is incorrect. The sentence provides information about making sunscreen and doesn't support sentence $\boxed{1}$.

C. Choice C is incorrect. The sentence provides information on easy-to-find sunscreen and doesn't support sentence $\boxed{1}$.

D. Choice D is incorrect. The sentence provides information about one type of lotion and doesn't support sentence $\boxed{1}$.

38. Which sentence below provides a detail that supports sentence ⑨?

   F.   Nutrients are needed from the sun.

   G.   For instance, vitamin D helps maintain a healthy immune system.

   H   Sun cream gives off nutrients.

   I.   The sun gives us certain nutrients.

Analysis:

F. Choice F is incorrect. This version of the sentence is a rewording of sentence ⑨.

G. Choice G is correct. This sentence provides a detail that supports sentence ⑨.

H. Choice H is incorrect. This sentence provides false information.

I. Choice I is incorrect. This sentence repeats information.

39. Read the sentence below from George's report:

> 13 **This was not very effective.**

Which word(s) should replace "This" in the sentence to make the wording most specific?

A. Using olive oil
B. Greeks
C. Greek and olive oil
D. Sunscreen

Analysis:

A. Choice A is correct. "Using olive oil" is the most specific information for the report.

B. Choice B is incorrect. "Greeks" and "was" do not have subject-verb agreement, and the sentence does not make sense.

C. Choice C is incorrect. "Greek and olive oil" and "was" do not have subject-verb agreement, and the sentence does not make sense.

D. Choice D is incorrect. "Sunscreen" is not specific enough.

40. Which sentence contains an unimportant detail that should be deleted from the report?

    F.   sentence $\boxed{12}$

    G.   sentence $\boxed{16}$

    H.   sentence $\boxed{17}$

    I.   sentence $\boxed{18}$

Analysis:

F. Choice F is incorrect. This sentence is the topic sentence for the fourth paragraph and provides focus for further details.

G. Choice G is incorrect. This sentence is the topic sentence of the last paragraph and helps direct the focus of the paragraph.

H. Choice H is incorrect. This sentence helps maintain focus and adds support to the main idea of the passage.

I. Choice I is correct. The detail provides information not related to the topic and does not maintain focus.

41. Read the sentence below from George's report:

> 6 **It attracts ultraviolet rays so you can become tan.**

Which revision below improves the word choice and removes the repetition from sentence 6 ?

A. Suntan lotion attracts ultraviolet rays so you can become tan.
B. The lotion attracts ultraviolet rays so you develop a tan.
C. To develop a tan, you should use it.
D. It causes you to become tan.

Analysis:

A. Choice A is incorrect. This sentence repeats what is said in sentence 6 and it repeats the use of the words "suntan lotion" that is already used in sentence 5.

B. Choice B is correct. This sentence is not repetitive and gives the reader a more specific idea of what suntan lotion will do when you use it.

C. Choice C is incorrect. This sentence is vague and does not explain the uses of the lotion.

D. Choice D is incorrect. This sentence is too vague.

The report below is a first draft that Lola wrote. The report contains errors. Read the report to answer questions 42—46.

Hermit Crabs Make Great Pets

1 Hermit crabs are a very low maintenance pet. 2 They almost take care of themselves. 3 They climb, dig, and tap on the glass of their "crabarium" when they want your attention. 4 To set up a "crabarium," you need a few essentials; gravel, sand, extra shells in different sizes, and shallow water and food dishes.

G

→   5 You do have to feed the hermit crabs daily. 6 It's very important to spray their cage with lukewarm water daily to keep the humidity level stable. 7 In addition to misting their cages, they do need drinking water. 8 Pet stores sell hermit crab food.

→   9 Hermit crabs have a hard exoskeleton that does not grow as the crab grows. 10 The crab has to shed its exoskeleton and move into a new shell. 11 They move into a new shell until the new exoskeleton hardens. 12 Then they shed the skin all over again.

13 This process is called molting.

14 Molting is a potentially dangerous period for a crab. 15
They become inactive, bury themselves, and give off a horrible
smell. 16 Depending on the size of the crab, the process can take
2—4 weeks. 17 Some crabs do die, because it is physically
draining on the crab to shed its skin. 18 Many owners believe their
crab has died when they are simply molting.

⟶ 　　　19 Once molting is complete, the hermit crab does two things.

20 It begins to eat the old exoskeleton. 21 The skin provides

nutrients the hermit crab needs to live for the next few months.

⟶ 　　　22 The second thing it does is look for a new shell.

23 Remember, they molt because they are too big for their skeleton

and their shell. 24 That is why they are called hermit crabs. 25

They move from place to place, and never stay in one home very

long.

42. Which transition should be added to the beginning of
    sentence $\boxed{20}$ to show the connection between ideas in the
    report?

    F. First
    G. However
    H. In addition to
    I. Finally

Analysis:

F. Choice F is correct. "First" indicates time order. Sentence [20] is the first of two separate pieces of information.

G. Choice G is incorrect. "However" indicates a counter example between sentences [19] and [20].

H. Choice H is incorrect. "In addition to" indicates additional information will be added in sentence [20].

I. Choice I is incorrect. "Finally" is not an appropriate transition from sentence [19] to [20] because sentence [20] is not the last sentence in the article.

43. Which sentence contains an unimportant detail that should be deleted from the report?

    A.   sentence 6

    B.   sentence 8

    C.   sentence 9

    D.   sentence 12

Analysis:

A. Choice A is incorrect. This is important to the report because this paragraph focuses on how you need to feed and water your hermit crab daily.

B. Choice B is correct. This sentence gives information about purchasing hermit crab food in a pet store and the paragraph is explaining how crabs shed their exoskeletons. This sentence is unimportant to the report.

C. Choice C is incorrect. This sentence explains about the crab's exoskeleton and is important to the central idea of the report.

D. Choice D is incorrect. This sentence is important to the report because it gives information about hermit crabs shedding their skin.

44. Which sentence below provides a detail that supports
    sentence 17 ?

    F.   The hermit crab will move from home to home.
    G.   You need to make sure that you have a good home for
         your new hermit crab.
    H.   The hermit crab will probably become lethargic, or
         tired.
    I.   When a hermit crab molts on the surface other hermit
         crabs may attack it.

Analysis:

F.   Choice F is incorrect. This sentence is about moving, not the physical condition of a hermit crab.

G.   Choice G is incorrect. This sentence is about making sure you have a good home for your crab.

H.   Choice H is correct. This sentence provides a detail that supports sentence $\boxed{17}$, which is about hermit crabs becoming physically drained due to molting.

I.   Choice I is incorrect. This sentence is about other crabs attacking a molting crab.

45. Which transition should be added to the beginning of
    sentence 10 to show the connection between ideas in the
    report?

    A. Still
    B. Finally
    C. Furthermore
    D. Therefore

Analysis:

A. Choice A is incorrect. "Still" is not an appropriate transition from sentence 9 to sentence 10.

B. Choice B is incorrect. "Finally" indicates time order and the action in the paragraph is not complete; in sentence 10 there is more action to follow.

C. Choice C is incorrect. "Furthermore" is not an appropriate transition from sentence 9 to sentence 10 because sentence 10 does not contain information that is an extension of sentence 9.

D. Choice D is correct. The transition "Therefore" indicates a result. The crab sheds its exoskeleton as a result of growing.

46. Lola wants to add the sentence below to her report.

> **However, you should supplement your hermit crab's diet with peanut butter, apples, and grains.**

Where should this sentence be added to keep the details in the correct order?

F. after sentence 8

G. after sentence 9

H. after sentence 10

I. after sentence 11

Analysis:

F.   Choice F is correct. Sentence $\boxed{8}$ tells the reader where to get hermit crab food. The detail of what should be supplemented into a crab's diet should follow this idea.

G.   Choice G is incorrect. Information about food would not follow sentence $\boxed{9}$, which is about the crab's exoskeleton.

H.   Choice H is incorrect. Information about food would not follow sentence $\boxed{10}$, which is about the crab shedding its exoskeleton.

I.   Choice I is incorrect. Information about food would not follow sentence $\boxed{11}$, which is about a crab moving into a new shell.

47. In which sentence below is all **punctuation** correct?

    A. Jorge dropped his hamburger; mustard splattered all over the floor.

    B. Jorge dropped his hamburger, mustard splattered all over the floor.

    C. Jorge dropped his hamburger mustard splattered all over the floor.

Analysis:

A. Choice A is correct. This choice shows the correct use of a semicolon to connect two sentences.

B. Choice B is incorrect. A comma is incorrect because a semicolon connects two complete thoughts with a longer pause than a comma.

C. Choice C is incorrect. The semicolon needed to connect these two sentences is missing.

48. Read the sentence below:

> **It's very important to read the directions
> before <u>they're test is administered.</u>**

Which type of error appears in the underlined section of
the sentence?

F. Capitalization error
G. Punctuation error
H. Usage error

Analysis:

F. Choice F is incorrect. No capitalization errors occur in the underlined section of this sentence.

G. Choice G is incorrect. No punctuation errors occur in the underlined section of this sentence.

H. Choice H is correct. "They're" is a contraction for "they are" and is not the correct form of the possessive pronoun "their."

49. Combine the ideas in the box to create one logical sentence.

> **had the**
> **over Niagara Falls**
> **the rainbow**
> **most vivid array of colors**

Which sentence below correctly combines the ideas from the box?

A. Over Niagara Falls, the rainbow had the most vivid array of colors.

B. The rainbow over Niagara Falls had the most vivid array of colors.

C. Most vivid array of colors, had the rainbow over Niagara Falls.

Analysis:
A. Choice A is incorrect. The order of words makes the meaning of the sentence confusing.

B. Choice B is correct. This sentence correctly combines the words in the box to create a complete and meaningful sentence.

C. Choice C is incorrect. The order of words makes the meaning of the sentence confusing.

50. Combine the ideas in the box to create one logical sentence.

> **soda and potato chips**
> **sandwich came with**
> **the bacon, lettuce, and tomato**

Which sentence below correctly combines the ideas from the box?

F. Soda and potato chips, the bacon, lettuce, and tomato sandwich came with.

G. Sandwich came with soda and potato chips; the bacon, lettuce, and tomato.

H. The bacon, lettuce, and tomato sandwich came with soda and potato chips.

Analysis:

F. Choice F is incorrect. The order of words makes the meaning of the sentence confusing.

G. Choice G is incorrect. The order of words makes the meaning of the sentence confusing.

H. Choice H is correct. This sentence correctly combines the words in the box to create a complete and meaningful sentence.

51. Read the sentence in the box.

> **Waiting in line at the amusement park, Gretchen
> did not hear her friend calling her.**

Which sentence below expresses the same meaning as the sentence in the box?

A. Gretchen did not hear her friend, waiting in line at the amusement park, calling her.

B. Her friend, waiting in line at the amusement park, did not hear Gretchen calling her.

C. Gretchen, waiting in line at the amusement park, did not hear her friend calling her.

Analysis:

A. Choice A is incorrect. This sentence states that her friend was waiting in line at the amusement park.

B. Choice B is incorrect. This sentence does not express the same idea as the original sentence.

C. Choice C is correct. This sentence rephrases the example sentence and maintains the original meaning.

52. Read the sentence in the box.

> **During his stay in Rome, Charles visited the Colosseum on a tour bus.**

Which sentence below expresses the same meaning as the sentence in the box?

F.   Charles, during his stay in Rome, visited the Colosseum on a tour bus.

G.   The tour bus visited the Colosseum, during Charles' stay in Rome.

H.   Charles, on a tour bus, visited the Colosseum during his stay.

Analysis:
F.   Choice F is correct. This sentence rephrases the example sentence and maintains the original meaning.

G.   Choice G is incorrect. This sentence does not express the same meaning as the example sentence.

H.   Choice H is incorrect. This sentence does not clearly express the meaning of the example sentence.

53. Combine the ideas in the box to create one logical sentence.

> **sat at the table**
> **and worked**
> **the two sisters**
> **on the jigsaw puzzle**

Which sentence below correctly combines the ideas from the box?

A. Sat at the table, the two sisters, and worked on the jigsaw puzzle.

B. The two sisters sat at the table and worked on the jigsaw puzzle.

C. On the jigsaw puzzle, the two sisters sat at the table and worked.

Analysis:
A. Choice A is incorrect. The order of words makes the meaning of the sentence confusing.

B. Choice B is correct. This sentence correctly combines the words in the box to create a complete and meaningful sentence.

C. Choice C is incorrect. The order of words makes the meaning of the sentence confusing.

The report below is a first draft that Arthur wrote for school. The report contains errors. Read the report to answer questions 54—58.

The American Red Cross

→ ⬚1 The American National Red Cross began in 1873 as a humanitarian effort providing medical aid during the Civil War by Clara Barton.

→ ⬚2 Her vacation in Europe became an introduction to the volunteer program for the International Red Cross during the Franco-Prussian War. ⬚3 She did not get much rest during that vacation.

→   4 President Chester A. Arthur was the first U.S. President,

after the Civil War, to support the American National Red Cross.

5 His administration wanted to expand the organization's

availability in response to national disasters other than massive

medical relief. 6 The American National Red Cross was given

money by John D. Rockefeller for a national building and built its

headquarters in Washington, D.C.

7 The Great Fire of 1881, in Thumb, Michigan, was the American National Red Cross's first disaster relief response effort led by Clara Barton. 8 She led two major relief efforts by 1900 and resigned as president in 1904. 9 She ended her presidency after two relief missions.

H

→ ⟦10⟧ The American National Red Cross is best known for its
collection of close to 45% of the United States' donated blood.

⟦11⟧ It is also known for its response to relief of natural disasters.

⟦12⟧ As a non-profit organization, volunteers run all of the programs
created by the Red Cross. ⟦13⟧ Some of the programs include baby-
sitting readiness, CPR training, life skills, swimming, and general
first aid practices.

→ ⟦14⟧ The American National Red Cross is now a part of the
International Red Cross and Red Crescent Societies.

54. Which sentence states information already presented and should be deleted from the report?

    F.   sentence 7

    G.   sentence 8

    H.   sentence 9

    I.   sentence 10

Analysis:

F. Choice F is incorrect. Sentence $\boxed{7}$ provides original information and is necessary to the text.

G. Choice G is incorrect. Sentence $\boxed{8}$ provides original information and is necessary to the text.

H. Choice H is correct. Sentence $\boxed{9}$ provides a detail that has already been presented and should be deleted.

I. Choice I is incorrect. Sentence $\boxed{10}$ provides original information and is necessary to the text.

55. Which transition should be added to the beginning of sentence 3 to show the connection between the ideas in the report?

     A.   Next
     B.   Finally
     C.   Consequently
     D.   First

Analysis:

A. Choice A is incorrect. "Next" does not connect the ideas in the report because the word "next" indicates time order.

B. Choice B is incorrect. "Finally" is not an appropriate transition from sentence ☐2 to sentence ☐3 because sentence ☐3 is not the last detail in the paper.

C. Choice C is correct. "Consequently" is the correct word to connect the ideas in the report because it indicates a cause/effect relationship.

D. Choice D is incorrect. "First" indicates time order and sentence ☐3 is not the first sentence in the paper.

56. Which sentence below should Arthur add to conclude the report?

   F.   The American National Red Cross' headquarters is located one block from the White House.

   G.   Clara Barton expanded the original concept of the Red Cross to include assisting in any great national disaster.

   H.   Barton finally succeeded in convincing President Arthur that the American National Red Cross could help in other types of crisis.

   I.   Thanks to Clara Barton, the United States has an organization dedicated to humanitarian disaster relief and emergency aid.

Analysis:

F. Choice F is incorrect. This is information about the headquarters. This would not be a conclusion to this report.

G. Choice G is incorrect. This is information about the expansion of the American National Red Cross not a conclusion.

H. Choice H is incorrect. This is information about the President and expansion of the American National Red Cross, not a conclusion to the report.

I. Choice I is correct. This would make a very good conclusion to this report because it is a summary of what was reported in the article.

57. Read the sentence below from Arthur's report:

> **14**   **The American National Red Cross is now a part of the International Federation of Red Cross and Red Crescent Societies.**

Which words should replace "is now a part of" in sentence **14** to make the wording more specific?

A. is presently a member of
B. now belongs to
C. is now in
D. is currently included in

Analysis:

A. Choice A is correct. "Is presently a member of" is more specific and clear than "is now part of."

B. Choice B is incorrect. "Now belongs to" is too vague.

C. Choice C is incorrect. "Is now in" is too vague.

D. Choice D is incorrect. "Is currently included in" is vague.

58. Arthur wants to add the sentence below to his report:

> **The search for missing soldiers during the Civil War physically exhausted Clara, so her doctor recommended a restful trip to Europe.**

Where should this sentence be added to keep the details in the correct order?

    F.   before sentence $\boxed{1}$

    G.   before sentence $\boxed{2}$

    H.   before sentence $\boxed{3}$

    I.   before sentence $\boxed{4}$

Analysis:

F. Choice F is incorrect. Sentence ①1① states the main idea of the article. Information about why Clara Barton was in Europe would not follow this sentence.

G. Choice G is correct. Sentence ②2② tells what happened on her vacation to Europe and this sentence explains why she was in Europe.

H. Choice H is incorrect. Sentence ③3③ tells the result of Clara Barton's vacation after being introduced to the International Red Cross.

I. Choice I is incorrect. Sentence ④4④ states what President Arthur did for the American National Red Cross and this sentence would not make sense to be placed before sentence ④4④.

59. In which sentence below is all **punctuation** correct?

    A.   This meal unlike my breakfast is very tasty.

    B.   This meal, unlike, my breakfast is very tasty.

    C.   This meal unlike my breakfast, is very tasty.

    D.   This meal, unlike my breakfast, is very tasty.

Analysis:

A. Choice A is incorrect. The commas to set off the parenthetical expression, or words to interrupt the sentence, are missing.

B. Choice B is incorrect. Only the word "unlike" is set off by commas.

C. Choice C is incorrect. There is only one comma in this sentence. The sentence needs a comma before "unlike" and after "breakfast."

D. Choice D is correct. The commas are in the correct location. They set off the parenthetical expression, or unnecessary words.

60. In which sentence is all **capitalization** correct?

   F.   My house is on the corner of Alhambra Road and
        Kipling Avenue.
   G.   My house is on the corner of alhambra Road and
        kipling Avenue.
   H.   My House is on the corner of Alhambra Road and
        Kipling Avenue.
   I.   My house is on the corner of Alhambra road and Kipling
        avenue.

Analysis:

F. Choice F is correct. "Alhambra Road" and "Kipling Avenue" are proper nouns that are capitalized.

G. Choice G is incorrect. "Alhambra Road" and "Kipling Avenue" are proper nouns that should be capitalized.

H. Choice H is incorrect. "House" is a common noun and should not be capitalized.

I. Choice I is incorrect. "Alhambra Road" and "Kipling Avenue" are proper nouns that should be capitalized.

Read the report "The History of MapQuest." Choose the word or words that correctly complete questions 61—66.

The History of MapQuest

MapQuest is owned by the Web Master, AOL. It can be accessed on the Web. MapQuest is free and easy to use. You simply type in the address of __(61)__ starting point.

The next address you type in __(62)__ your final destination. A numbered list pops up with right and left turns, detailed street __(63)__, distance traveled, and time traveled on that road.

I

It also gives you a regular map (64) look at and follow. In 2006, MapQuest created technology allowing (65) users to add extra stops. MapQuest is very helpful when you do not know where you are going.

I

61. Which answer should go in blank (61)?

    A. your
    B. you're
    C. yore

Analysis:
A. Choice A is correct because it shows possession of the "starting point."

B. Choice B is incorrect because "you're" is the contraction for "you are."

C. Choice C is incorrect because "yore" means "long ago."

I61

62. Which answer should go in blank (62)?

    F.   is
    G.   was
    H.   were

Analysis:

F.   Choice F is correct because the singular verb "is" agrees with the singular subject "you."

G.   Choice G is incorrect because the singular verb "was" does not agree with the singular subject "you."

H.   Choice H is incorrect because the singular verb "were" does not make sense in the sentence.

63. Which answer should go in blank (63)?

   A.   name's
   B.   names
   C.   names'

Analysis:

A. Choice A is incorrect because "name's" is possessive.

B. Choice B is correct because "names" is a common noun.

C. Choice C is incorrect because "names'" is possessive plural.

I63

64. Which answer should go in blank (64)?

     F.   to
     G.   two
     H.   too

Analysis:

F.   Choice F is correct because "to" is the preposition necessary for the sentence.

G.   Choice G is incorrect because "two" is a number.

H.   Choice H is incorrect because "too" is an adverb adding "much or little" to a sentence.

65. Which answer should go in blank (65)?

    A.   it's
    B.   its
    C.   its'

Analysis:

A. Choice A is incorrect because "it's" is the contraction for "it is."

B. Choice B is correct because "its" is a pronoun.

C. Choice C is incorrect because "its'" is the possessive plural of the pronoun.

66. Read the sentence below:

<u>The outfit always looks more better on the model</u> walking down the runway than on the person who buys it.

What type of error appears in the underlined section of the sentence?

F. Usage error
G. Capitalization error
H. Punctuation error

Analysis:
F. Choice F is correct because "more better" is the incorrect use of the comparative for "good, better, best."

G. Choice G is incorrect because there are no capitalization errors.

H. Choice H is incorrect because there are no punctuation errors.

67. In which sentence is all **usage** correct?

   A. There are studies proving that children who eat
       breakfast do better on standardized tests.
   B. There are studies proving that children whom eat
       breakfast do better on standardized tests.
   C. There are studies proving that children that eat
       breakfast do better on standardized tests.

Analysis:

A. Choice A is correct because "who" is the correct pronoun for the noun "children."

B. Choice B is incorrect because "whom" is an objective form of the pronoun "who."

C. Choice C is incorrect because "that" is a pronoun used when referring to things or objects, not children.

Read the report "Oktoberfest." Choose the word or words that correctly complete questions 68—72.

Oktoberfest

The Oktoberfest in Sarasota, Fla., has been a record-setting event for years. In 2005, 15,000 people __(68)__ the festival located inside of Sarasota County's Fairgrounds. __(69)__ the festival is held during the first and second weekends in October.

J

There, food vendors, musicians, and people looking to celebrate German culture come together for the party of the year. An event for the whole family, Oktoberfest _(70)_ free admission to attendees who wear authentic German dress.

One of the _(71)_ popular things about the festival however,
is the food. There are cooking lessons each weekend for anyone
who wants to learn to make potato pancakes, Wiener Schnitzel, or
Bavarian cheesecake.

_(72)_ the musicians who perform at the festival are one of a
kind. Many bands perform all over the world. This year, a band from
Austria is expected to bring their European sound to Sarasota.

Definition: Cloze Selections

Cloze selections are passages with numbered blanks that specifically test the conventions of spelling and usage.

They contain high-interest material in a relatively short format that can be more literary or technical in nature than the text in the other sample types.

On the FCAT Writing+ for Grade 8, cloze selections may range from 75—350 words.

68. Which answer should go in blank (68)?

    F.   attends

    G. attended

    H. attending

Analysis:

F.   Choice F is incorrect. "Attends" is not the correct verb tense for this sentence.

G.   Choice G is correct. "Attended" is the correct verb tense for this sentence because the record-setting attendance happened in 2005.

H.   Choice H is incorrect. "Attending" is not the correct verb tense for this sentence.

69. Which answer should go in blank (69)?

    A. Annully
    B. Annualy
    C. Annually

Analysis:

A. Choice A is incorrect because "annully" is spelled incorrectly.

B. Choice B is incorrect because "annualy" is spelled incorrectly.

C. Choice C is correct because "annually" is spelled correctly.

70. Which answer should go in blank (70)?

    F.   offers

    G. offered

    H. offering

Analysis:

F. Choice F is correct. "Offers" is the correct present tense form of the verb "offer."

G. Choice G is incorrect. "Offered" is the past-tense form of the verb "offer" and incorrectly applied in this sentence.

H. Choice H is incorrect. The use of the verb "offering" in this sentence is not proper English.

71. Which answer should go in blank (71)?

   A. mostest
   B. most
   C. much

Analysis:

A. Choice A is incorrect because "mostest" is not a word.

B. Choice B is correct because "most" is the correct adjective for this sentence.

C. Choice C is incorrect because "much" is not the correct adjective to use in this sentence.

72. Which answer should go in blank (72)?

   F.   First
   G.   Lastly
   H.   Next

Analysis:

F. Choice F is incorrect. The transition "first" indicates time order and is improper for use in the last paragraph of the report.

G. Choice G is correct. The transition "lastly" indicates that this is the last topic discussed in this report.

H. Choice H is incorrect. The transition "next" indicates that additional information will be added after this information.

73. In which sentence below is all **spelling** correct?

    A. It is best to go fishing befour sunrise, because you're
       more likely to catch a fish.

    B. It is best to go fishing befoor sunrise, because you're
       more likely to catch a fish.

    C. It is best to go fishing before sunrise, because you're
       more likely to catch a fish.

Analysis:

A. Choice A is incorrect. "Befour" is not the correct spelling of the preposition.

B. Choice B is incorrect. "Befoor" is not the correct spelling of the preposition.

C. Choice C is correct. "Before" is the correct spelling of the preposition.

74. In which sentence below is all **capitalization** correct?

F. The student's book bag was so heavy, she could barely carry it into school on tuesday.

G. The student's book bag was so heavy, she could barely carry it into School on Tuesday.

H. The student's book bag was so heavy, she could barely carry it into school on Tuesday.

Analysis:

F. Choice F is incorrect. The sentence contains a day of the week, which must be capitalized.

G. Choice G is incorrect. "School" is not a proper noun and should not be capitalized.

H. Choice H is correct. "Tuesday" is the only proper noun in the sentence and must be capitalized.

75. Read the sentence below:

> **The <u>painting company came to make an estimite</u> for painting the inside of the whole house, but no one was home.**

Which type of error appears in the underlined section of the sentence?

A. Punctuation error
B. Spelling error
C. Usage error

Analysis:

A.   Choice A is incorrect. There are no punctuation errors in this sentence.

B.   Choice B is correct. The correct spelling is "estimate," not "estimite."

C.   Choice C is incorrect. There are no usage errors in this sentence.

76. In which sentence below is all **usage** correct?

F. Jessica has ate all of her dinner, even though she had a
    stomachache.
G. Jessica eaten all of her dinner, even though she had a
    stomachache.
H. Jessica ate all of her dinner, even though she had a
    stomachache.

Analysis:

F. Choice F is incorrect. The verb "has ate" is the incorrect verb form.

G. Choice G is incorrect. The verb "eaten" is the incorrect verb form.

H. Choice H is correct. "Ate" is the correct past-tense verb form.

77. In which sentence is all **spelling** correct?

   A. The peaces of the puzzle did not match the cover on
      the box, so it was difficult to put it together.
   B. The pieces of the puzzle did not match the cover on
      the box, so it was difficult to put it together.
   C. The peices of the puzzle did not match the cover on
      the box, so it was difficult to put it together.

Analysis:

A. Choice A is incorrect because "peaces" means freedom from war.

B. Choice B is correct because "pieces" are the parts of the puzzle.

C. Choice C is incorrect because "peices" incorrectly applies the spelling rule of placing an "i before e except after c."

78. Read the sentence in the box.

> **<u>Dress rehearsal for the musical _The Wizard of Oz_</u> is scheduled for 3:00 p.m., Thursday.**

What type of error appears in the underlined section of the sentence?

F. Usage error
G. Punctuation error
H. Spelling error

Analysis:

F. Choice F is incorrect because there are no usage errors in the sentence.

G. Choice G is correct because *The Wizard of Oz* adds additional information to the sentence and should be set off by a pair of commas.

H. Choice H is incorrect because there are no spelling errors in the sentence.

79. Read the sentence below:

Monday evening, a tornado went whirling threw Orange County.

What type of error appears in the underlined section of the sentence?

A. Capitalization error
B. Usage error
C. Punctuation error

Analysis:
A.   Choice A is incorrect. There are no capitalization errors in this sentence.

B.   Choice B is correct. The correct use is "through," not "threw."

C.   Choice C is incorrect. There are no punctuation errors in this sentence.

80. Read the sentence below:

**<u>That was the most funniest</u> Broadway
show I have ever seen.**

What type of error appears in the underlined section of the sentence?

F.   Punctuation error
G.   Capitalization error
H.   Usage error

Analysis:
F. Choice F is incorrect. There are no punctuation errors in this sentence.

G. Choice G is incorrect. There are no capitalization errors in this sentence.

H. Choice H is correct. "Most funniest" is the incorrect form of the superlative, "funniest."

81. Combine the ideas in the box to create one logical sentence.

> **you can do**
> **all of your clothes shopping**
> **for the most part**
> **at the local mall**

Which sentence below correctly combines the ideas from the box?

A. You can do, for the most part, at the local mall, all of your clothes shopping.

B. For the most part, you can do all of your clothes shopping at the local mall.

C. At the local mall, for the most part, you can do, all of our clothes shopping.

Analysis:

A. Choice A is incorrect. The order of words makes the meaning of the sentence confusing.

B. Choice B is correct. This sentence correctly combines the words in the box to create a complete and meaningful sentence.

C. Choice C is incorrect. The order of words makes the meaning of the sentence confusing.

82. Read the sentence below:

**The author and illustrator of the <u>comic strip
 is two different people.</u>**

What type of error appears in the underlined section of the
sentence?

F. Capitalization error
G. Usage error
H. Punctuation error

Analysis:

F.   Choice F is incorrect. This sentence has no capitalization errors.

G.   Choice G is correct. The singular form of the verb "is" does not agree with the plural form of the subject "author and illustrator."

H.   Choice H is incorrect. This sentence has no punctuation errors.

83. Combine the ideas in the box to create one logical sentence.

> **Gabriel and Rita like to eat candy apples**
> **They eat candy apples at the State Fair**
> **When they go with their friends**

Which sentence below correctly combines the ideas from the box?

A. Gabriel and Rita like candy apples with their friends at the State Fair.

B. Gabriel and Rita like to eat candy apples at the State Fair with their friends.

C. Gabriel and Rita like the state fair when they go with their friends and eat candy apples.

Analysis:
A. Choice A is incorrect. This is not a logical sentence.

B. Choice B is correct. This sentence correctly combines the ideas in the box to create one complete sentence.

C. Choice C is incorrect. This sentence is not logical and changes the meaning of the ideas in the box.

Read the report "The Smart Young Actor." Choose the word or words that correctly complete questions 84—89.

The Smart Young Actor

The (84) speech the famous child actor gave was entertaining and heartfelt. He thanked everyone in a very short amount of time. It (85) best speech of the evening.

K

When his speech was over, he invited everyone over to his mansion for a peace of cake and ice cream. (86), when the guests (87) at the (88), there was no cake. The actor "acted" quickly, and ordered pizza for everyone. Every slice of pizza was (89) before midnight when all the guests went home.

K

84. Which answer should go in blank (84)?

    F. acceptance
    G. axceptance
    H. acceptince

Analysis:

F. Choice F is correct. This is the correct spelling of the word "acceptance."

G. Choice G is incorrect. "Axceptance" is an incorrect spelling of the word "acceptance."

H. Choice H is incorrect. "Acceptince" is an incorrect spelling of the word "acceptance."

85. Which answer should go in blank (85)?

A. was

B. is

C. are

Analysis:

A. Choice A is correct. "Was" is correct because it is past tense.

B. Choice B is incorrect. "Is" is present tense.

C. Choice C is incorrect. "Are" is present tense and plural.

86. Which answer should go in blank (86)?

   F. However
   G. Finally
   H. Therefore

Analysis:

F. Choice F is correct. "However" presents a contrast to the previous sentence.

G. Choice G is incorrect. "Finally" is not an appropriate transition for this sentence.

H. Choice H is incorrect. "Therefore" is not an appropriate transition for this sentence.

87. Which answer should go in blank (87)?

   A. arrive
   B. arrived
   C. arriving

Analysis:
A. Choice A is incorrect. "Arrive" is present tense and this sentence is in past tense.

B. Choice B is correct. "Arrived" is past tense.

C. Choice C is incorrect. "Arriving" is a present participle.

88. Which answer should go in blank (88)?

   F.   manson
   G.   mantion
   H.   mansion

Analysis:
F.   Choice F is incorrect. The correct spelling is "mansion," not "manson."

G.   Choice G is incorrect. The correct spelling is "mansion," not "mantion."

H.   Choice H is correct. This is the correct spelling of the word "mansion."

89. Which answer should go in blank (89)?

   A.   aten
   B.   eatin
   C.   eaten

Analysis:

A. Choice A is incorrect. This is the incorrect spelling of the word "eaten."

B. Choice B is incorrect. This is the incorrect spelling of the word "eaten."

C. Choice C is correct. "Eaten" is the correct spelling.

The report below is a first draft that Marguerite wrote for school. The report contains errors. Read the report to answer questions 90—96.

The Giant Panda

1 The Giant panda is found in southwest China in damp forests full of bamboo. 2 The Giant panda is China's "national treasure" and is revered by most of the world. 3 The Chinese have used them in their art as symbols of royalty for thousands of years.

L

→ 4 Father P'ere Armand David, a French Missionary, gave the first description of the pandas to the outside world in 1869. 5 Since then, the world has remained under the Giant panda's spell. 6 China and the rest of the world collaborate to help keep the pandas from becoming extinct.

→ 7 Bamboo, their primary source of food and shelter, is one of the reasons why pandas are endangered. 8 Bamboo is a slow growing plant and the pandas primary source of food and shelter.

9 Once the plant reaches the flowering stage and produces seeds, the plant dies. 10 Pandas will not eat dead bamboo. 11 They can eat up to 25 different types of bamboo. 12 Once the bamboo dies in their region, they move on. 13 This strange growth cycle, plus an increase in human population, is decreasing the amount of food for the pandas.

L

14 Giant pandas were thought to be a part of the raccoon family at one time. 15 Scientists recently confirmed they were related to the bear family. 16 They have the same abilities to walk and climb, the same body shape, and the same skull.

→ 17 Baby pandas are born very small; they need their mother's undivided attention. 18 Usually, the female panda gives birth to one or two panda cubs. 19 She is only able to care for one of her cubs. 20 She usually abandons one of her cubs, and it dies soon after birth. 21 This is another reason pandas are at risk for extinction.

→   [22] Only 1,600 Giant pandas are left on planet Earth. [23] In
addition to habitat shortage and high infant death, hunting and
trapping is another problem. [24] Hunters who are setting traps for
other animals often find a panda instead.

→   [25] They are working around the clock to save the Giant
panda!

90. Read the sentence below from Marguerite's report:

> 13   **This strange growth cycle, plus an increase in human population, is decreasing the amount of food for the pandas.**

Which word(s) should replace the word "This" in the sentence to make the wording more specific?

F. Bamboo's
G. Panda's
H. China's
I. Bamboo's and Panda's

Analysis:

F. Choice F is correct because "Bamboo's" is the most specific wording to replace the pronoun "This" in this sentence.

G. Choice G is incorrect. "Panda's" does not make sense in this sentence because it does not maintain the same meaning.

H. Choice H is incorrect. "China's" does not make sense in this sentence because it does not maintain the same meaning.

I. Choice I is incorrect. "Bamboo's and Panda's" does not make sense in this sentence because it does not maintain the same meaning.

91. Which sentence states information already presented and should be deleted from the report?

   A.   sentence 6

   B.   sentence 7

   C.   sentence 8

   D.   sentence 9

Analysis:

A.   Choice A is incorrect. This sentence states that the world is working toward helping pandas from becoming extinct.

B.   Choice B is correct. This sentence states that pandas are endangered and that bamboo is a primary source of their food. This information is repeated in sentences $\boxed{6}$ and $\boxed{8}$. This sentence can be deleted.

C.   Choice C is incorrect. This sentence states that bamboo is slow growing and that it is the primary source of food for the panda.

D.   Choice D is incorrect. This sentence is about how bamboo grows and dies and is necessary to the rest of the report.

92. Marguerite wants to add the sentence below to her article:

> **Although the species is still endangered, it is thought that the conservation efforts are working.**

Where should this sentence be added to keep the details in the correct order?

F. before sentence 22

G. before sentence 23

H. before sentence 24

I. before sentence 25

Analysis:

F. Choice F is incorrect. Sentence $\boxed{22}$ tells how many pandas are left on Earth and sentence $\boxed{23}$ further explains this.

G. Choice G is incorrect. Sentence $\boxed{23}$ gives appropriate details related to sentence $\boxed{22}$.

H. Choice H is incorrect. Sentence $\boxed{24}$ states that hunters are setting traps for pandas. This sentence would not follow a sentence about conservation.

I. Choice I is correct. Sentence $\boxed{25}$ states that "they," meaning the scientists and conservationists, are working around the clock to save the giant panda. This sentence would give a detail about the conservation effort.

COPYING IS PROHIBITED   L92

93. Which transition should be added to the beginning of sentence $\boxed{22}$?

   A. Therefore
   B. For example
   C. Next
   D. Despite

Analysis:

A. Choice A is incorrect. "Therefore" indicates a cause/effect relationship that is not present.

B. Choice B is correct. "For example" indicates supplemental ideas are being added to the information in sentence $\boxed{21}$.

C. Choice C is incorrect. "Next" indicates time order.

D. Choice D is incorrect. "Despite" indicates a contrast to information.

94. Why does Marguerite present her report the way she does?

F. She wants to compare the different types of pandas to show how they are alike.

G. She wants to show how important pandas are to the world and what is causing their risk for extinction.

H. She wants to emphasize that without help from conservationists the panda will become extinct.

I. She wants to present the most important detail about the panda first and then give her opinion about the panda population.

Analysis:

F. Choice F is incorrect. She is not comparing different types of pandas in this report.

G. Choice G is correct. Organizing her report as a cause-and-effect would be appropriate for showing what is happening to the pandas today.

H. Choice H is incorrect. She does mention that conservationists can help the pandas but this is not the focus of the report.

I. Choice I is incorrect. This is not an opinion report.

95. Which sentence below provides a detail that supports sentence 17?

A. Baby pandas weigh only 90 to 130 grams (3.2 to 4.6 ounces) at birth.

B. They may eat other foods such as honey, eggs, fish, and yams.

C. Scientists do not know how the female chooses which cub to raise.

D. The giant panda does not hibernate.

Analysis:

A. Choice A is correct. This sentence provides a detail to support sentence $\boxed{17}$, which is about the size of giants pandas when they are born.

B. Choice B is incorrect. This sentence is about eating habits.

C. Choice C is incorrect. This sentence is about the female panda choosing which cub to raise.

D. Choice D is incorrect. This sentence is about hibernating.

96. Read the sentence below from Marguerite's report:

 They are working around the clock and around the world to save the Giant Panda!

Which word(s) should replace "They" in the sentence to make the wording most specific?

F. Scientists

G. Giant pandas

H. Pandas

I. Scientists and pandas

Analysis:

F. Choice F is correct. "Scientists" is the most specific answer to replace the pronoun "They."

G. Choice G is incorrect. "Giant Pandas" does not make sense in the sentence because it does not maintain the same meaning.

H. Choice H is incorrect. "Pandas" does not make sense in this sentence because it does not maintain the same meaning.

I. Choice I is incorrect because "Scientists and pandas" does not make sense in this sentence because it does not maintain the same meaning.

Expository Writing Prompt

Below is an example of an expository prompt. The purpose of expository writing is to explain, define, or tell how to do something by giving information. The first part of the prompt presents the topic: allowance. The second part suggests that you think about why it is important for teenagers to receive an allowance.

Writing Situation:

> *Most teenagers receive an allowance.*

Directions for Writing:

> *Think about why it is important for a teenager to receive an allowance.*
>
> *Now write to explain why it is important for a teenager to receive an allowance.*

I think that it is very important for teenagers to receive an allowance from their parents. The major reason why it is extremely important for teenagers to receive an allowance is so they can learn how to manage their money.

Most teenagers do not start working until they are 16 years old. And when they do get a job, many do not know what to do with their paychecks and spend them all at the mall.

By receiving an allowance before starting a job, a teenager can learn how to save their money for the things they really want in the future, for example, a car.

An allowance does not have to be a large amount of money, just enough to allow teens the chance to understand how managing money works, and how important it is to be responsible with a paycheck.

Persuasive Writing Prompt

Below is an example of a persuasive prompt. The purpose of persuasive writing is to convince the reader to accept your opinion or to take a specific action. The first part of the prompt focuses on spring break in Italy. The second part suggests that you think about the importance of allowing the eighth grade to go to Italy, and then write to persuade your school administrator to accept your point of view.

Writing Situation:

>   *Your school is considering allowing the eighth grade to go to Italy as a class trip during spring break.*

>   *Think about why it is important for the eighth grade to go to Italy.*

Directions for Writing:

>   *Compose a letter to your school administrators persuading them to allow your eighth-grade class to go to Venice, Italy, during spring break.*

Dear Superintendent Mitchell,

I believe that allowing our eighth-grade class the opportunity to go to Venice, Italy, for spring break will be an unforgettable and once-in-a-lifetime experience.

In recent months, the eighth grade has been learning about the history and culture of Italy. We have even learned to say words like "ciao," which means both "hello" and "good-bye." I think that taking our learning experience out of the classroom and actually into that country would be invaluable.

Many students and their families do not get to travel much, especially overseas. By allowing the eighth-grade class this chance of a lifetime, the school will be opening up all of the students' minds.

Thank you very much.

> Sincerely,
> Suzie Maloney, eighth-grade student

Show What You Know® on the FCAT

Test-Preparation Products

Workbooks

Show What You Know® on the 3rd Grade FCAT
Show What You Know® on the 4th Grade FCAT
Show What You Know® on the 4th Grade FCAT, Writing+
Show What You Know® on the 5th Grade FCAT
Show What You Know® on the FCAT Mathematics for Grade 6
Show What You Know® on the FCAT Reading for Grade 6
Show What You Know® on the FCAT Mathematics for Grade 7
Show What You Know® on the FCAT Reading for Grade 7
Show What You Know® on the FCAT Mathematics for Grade 8
Show What You Know® on the FCAT Reading for Grade 8
Show What You Know® on the FCAT Language Arts for Grade 8
Show What You Know® on the FCAT Science for Grade 8
Show What You Know® on the FCAT Mathematics for Grade 9
Show What You Know® on the FCAT Reading for Grade 9
Show What You Know® on the FCAT Mathematics for Grade 10
Show What You Know® on the FCAT Reading for Grade 10
Show What You Know® on the FCAT Language Arts for Grade 10
Show What You Know® on the FCAT Science for Grade 11

Flash Cards

Show What You Know® Mathematics, Grades 3-5
Show What You Know® Reading, Grades 3-5
Show What You Know® Writing+, Grade 4
Show What You Know® Mathematics, Grades 6-8
Show What You Know® Reading, Grades 6-8
Show What You Know® Writing+, Grade 8
Show What You Know® Science, Grade 8
Show What You Know® Mathematics, Grades9-10
Show What You Know® Reading, Grades 9-10
Show What You Know® Writing+, Grade 10
Show What You Know® Science, Grade 11

Call 1-877-PASSING (727-7464) toll free.
Order online at: www.passthefcat.com

Item # FL5816

Show What You Know® on the FCAT Writing+ Flash Cards for Grade 8

This deck of flash cards features important concepts tested by the Florida Comprehensive Assessment Test (FCAT) in Writing. The deck includes 12 passage cards, 96 cards with questions and answers, 2 writing-prompt cards, and 4 information cards.

- Students can practice with multiple-choice questions and writing prompts.
- All questions are perfectly correlated to the Sunshine State Standards and Benchmarks.
- Questions are designed to review important concepts tested by the FCAT.
- Question analysis is given on the back of each card.
- These flash cards can be used for quizzes, assessment, homework, and student self-study.
- Coated card stock provides durability.

51495

ISBN 1-59230-233-5

9 781592 302338

$14.95

© 2006 Englefield & Associates, Inc.
Show What You Know® Publishing
Educational Publishers, Specializing in Test-Preparation Materials
Printed in the U.S.A.